GANDHI
Through a Child's Eyes

An Intimate Memoir

By Narayan Desai

Translated by Bhal Malji
Edited by Mark Shepard

A Peacewatch Edition

Ocean Tree Books • Santa Fe

An Ocean Tree Peacewatch Edition

OCEAN TREE BOOKS
Post Office Box 1295
Santa Fe, New Mexico 87504

Also in this series:
  Gandhi's Seven Steps to Global Change
  The Great Peace March: An American Odyssey
  Mikhail Gorbachev / A Road to the Future

This is an abridgment of *Bliss Was It to Be Young—
With Gandhi: Childhood Reminiscences,* Bharatiya Vidya
Bhavan, Bombay, 1988. (A Gujarati language edition was
published by Balgovind Prakashan, Ahmedabad, 1967.)

Printed in the United States of America.

Cover and text design by Simple Productions.
Front cover photo by Kanu Gandhi.

ISBN 0–943734–23–1
Library of Congress CIP Data:

```
Desai, Narayan.
    Gandhi through a child's eyes : an intimate memoir / by Narayan
Desai ; translated by Bhal Malji ; edited by Mark Shepard.
        p.    cm. -- (A Peacewatch edition)
    Includes index.
    ISBN 0-943734-23-1
    1. Gandhi, Mahatma, 1869-1948.  2. Statesmen--India--Biography.
3. Nationalists--India--Biography.  4. Desai, Narayan--Childhood and
youth.  5. Social workers--India--Biography.  [1. Gandhi, Mahatma,
1869-1948.  2. Statesmen.  3. Desai, Narayan--Childhood and youth.]
I. Desai, Narayan.  Bliss, was it to be young-- with Gandhi.
II. Title.  III. Series.
DS481.G3D442  1991
954.03'5'092--dc20
[B]                                                    91-18127
```

Contents

Introduction

by Mark Shepard

I first met Narayan Desai in 1978, at a cafeteria table in the dining hall of the Gandhi Peace Foundation in New Delhi. At first, I didn't catch his name. So I was happily surprised when I found I was talking with one of the top figures in the Gandhian movement.

I was privileged to spend time with Narayan on several occasions while in India. I came to greatly admire this charming, sincere, thoughtful man. I also grew to see him as an embodiment of the Gandhian tradition.

It's not surprising, when you consider his background. Narayan's father was Mahadev Desai, chief secretary to Mahatma Gandhi from 1917 until Desai's death in 1942. Narayan, born in 1924, spent his first twenty years in Gandhi's ashrams—the experience on which these memoirs are based.

Narayan also has been involved in Gandhian activities ever since. For many years, he taught at a school for "basic education," Gandhi's system using practical work as a springboard to all other knowledge. In the 1950s, he walked

Mark Shepard is the author of *Gandhi Today* and *The Community of the Ark*.

8,000 miles through India's villages collecting donations of land for the poor, as part of the Gandhians' "Land Gift" campaign.

From 1962 to 1974, Narayan directed Shanti Sena, the Gandhian "Peace Army," combatting urban riots with active nonviolence and conducting relief work for victims of war and natural disaster. In 1974, he was a major organizer in the "JP Movement," which later led to Indira Gandhi's declaration of Emergency and her 1977 electoral defeat.*

After the Emergency, Narayan was a prime figure among the Gandhians, developing training programs and organizing "people's committees" to watchdog the government. In 1982, he founded the Institute for Total Revolution, where he today trains a new generation of Gandhian social and political activists.** He has also helped launch a movement opposing India's nuclear power program.

Internationally, Narayan has contributed to a number of peacemaking efforts. In 1981, he helped found a new world organization called Peace Brigades International, which he co-directs.*** In 1988, he was elected chairman of War Resisters International, a world network devoted to active nonviolence. He is today frequently called upon to travel to other countries to share his expertise and his stories.

---

*Narayan's role in Shanti Sena and the JP movement are described in my *Gandhi Today* (Simple Productions and Seven Locks Press).

**Institute for Total Revolution, Vedchhi, Dt. Surat, Gujarat 394 641, India.

***Peace Brigades International, Woolman Hill, Keets Road, Deerfield, Massachusetts 01342, USA.

Narayan's memoirs provide a rare insider's look, not only at Gandhi, but also at life in Gandhi's ashrams. Traditionally, an *ashram* is a religious community, similar to a monastery in the West. But, for Gandhi, it was also a center of political and social action, as well as a laboratory for experiments in utopian living.

Gandhi's first major ashram in India was Sabarmati Ashram, located across the Sabarmati River from the city of Ahmedabad, in Gandhi's home province of Gujarat in western India. He founded it in 1917, two years after returning to India from South Africa, and remained there until 1930. It was from this ashram that he began his famous Salt March—a simple, ingenious act that led to the disruption of British rule throughout the country and forced Britain for the first time to negotiate with India as an equal.

After the Salt March campaign, Gandhi arranged for the ashram to be used as a development center for Harijans (the name Gandhi gave to India's "untouchables"). But, after Gandhi's death, the free government of India converted the main grounds into a memorial.

In 1933, Gandhi moved his base from Sabarmati to the city of Wardha, near the very center of India. His headquarters there was a donated estate he renamed Maganwadi, after his deceased nephew, Maganlal.

In 1936, he moved again, to the nearby village of Segaon, which he renamed *Sevagram*—"Service Village." A new ashram sprang up next to the village. Sevagram Ashram remained Gandhi's base until his death in 1948—though after 1942 he seldom stayed there.

Today, Gandhians still engage in social work in the

area around the ashram, but this ashram too is itself a memorial. The original buildings are maintained much as they were at Gandhi's death by a small number of elderly residents, including several who lived there in Gandhi's time.

A few facts about Indian forms of address will help keep names straight.

Common titles of respect placed before the name include *Shri* ("Mr."), *Shrimati* ("Mrs."), *Pandit* ("Dr."), and *Acharya* ("Professor"). *Mahatma* itself is a title, meaning "Great Soul."

Besides such titles, Indians often attach suffixes to names to show affection or respect. A suffix commonly used to indicate both is *–ji,* as in "Gandhiji." Also, Gandhians in India commonly call each other "Brother" and "Sister" by adding to each other's names the suffixes *–bhai* (pronounced like "by") and *–ben,* as in "Mahadevbhai" and "Anasuyaben."

Because of such conventions, a person's name might appear in more than one form. What's more, Indian children receive both a formal name, and an informal one for use by family and close friends. Within these memoirs, the author is known as *Babla.*

Gandhi himself was called *Bapu*—"Father"—by his associates. (Because of this, Narayan wound up calling his own father "Uncle.") Gandhi's wife Kasturbai was called *Ba*—"Mother." However, Kasturbai was also often called *Kasturba,* a shorthand version for "Mother Kasturbai."

Narayan Desai is not only a foremost exponent of the Gandhian tradition—he is also an accomplished writer and a master storyteller. So it has been both privilege and pleasure to edit these memoirs for the sake of Western readers.

I hope you find them as delightful and enlightening as I have.

1

Sabarmati Ashram

The site of Sabarmati Ashram has a significance of its own. It is said that somewhere near here, ages ago, stood the ashram of Dadhichi, the hermit who gave up his bones to be made into a thunderbolt for god Indra.

The story of Dadhichi is an example of supreme sacrifice. But the story of the Mahatma who built his ashram here in modern times is no less inspiring.

"This is a good spot for my ashram," Bapu* used to say. "On one side is the cremation ground. On the other is the prison. The people in my ashram should have no fear of death, nor should they be strangers to imprisonment."

One of us would chime in, "Yes, Bapu, and across the river are the chimneys of the textile mills, reminding us of the forces we must contend with, as advocates of khadi."**

---

*"Father." Gandhi's name among his close associates.

**"Homespun cloth." Gandhi promoted khadi to stop the flow of wealth from India's villages to Britain and to India's cities, and also to provide employment for the most destitute.

My earliest memories of Bapu are intertwined with those of Sabarmati Prison.

Bapu would go for a walk each morning and evening. He would put his hands on the shoulders of those to either side. These companions would be Bapu's "walking sticks." We children were always given top choice for this job.

Whether his human walking sticks were really any help to him, perhaps only Bapu could say. But, as for us, being chosen always made us swell with pride. In fact, in our eagerness to be chosen, Bapu's "sticks" would sometimes clash.

Each morning and evening, we would start out from Bapu's place, walk to the main gate of Sabarmati Prison, then turn back. At any time, Bapu's pace was too brisk for us. But, as we neared the prison gate—if he wasn't engaged in serious discussion—he would almost run the last fifty yards or so.

Sometimes we would remove Bapu's hands from our shoulders and dash to the gate. Sometimes Bapu would put his entire weight on our shoulders, lift his feet off the ground and shout, "Come on, Boss, let's see how you run!"

Bapu used to nickname those he cared about, often bestowing more than one name. Among the many showered on me was "Boss." Of course, he meant it in fun, and at that age it certainly never aroused in me the quality implied.

Experiments in the ashram encompassed every aspect of life. Naturally, this included health. In its pursuit, quite a few factors were taken into account.

Regularity and restraint were important rules of ashram

life. We stayed close to nature. Standard medical practice had been set aside, replaced by experimental, natural treatments. Different types of bath were tried. Mud packs on the head and abdomen were advocated by some.

Above all, Bapu liked to experiment with diet. If an ashramite wanted to try a special diet, Bapu would go all out to encourage it. Some would eat only raw food, others would drink peanut milk, still others would take to bitter neem leaves.

What was amazing was that Bapu was an expert adviser in all these fields of experiment. But, in the midst of them all, the best medicines were always Bapu's personal care, his faith, his sense of humor. In fact, you could say that illness here was a boon, since it was rewarded with two visits a day from Bapu.

Though Bapu paid special attention to the sick, he also kept close contact with every person in the ashram. He maintained a deep interest in their diet and living conditions. In every aspect of their individual or collective discipline, Bapu guided them directly or indirectly.

In this way, Bapu could be seen as the patriarch of a large, extended family. Certainly the ashram was a patriarchy. But my personal view of Bapu—and I believe the view of the other ashram children—was completely different. Bapu was father to the ashram, leader of the nation, Mahatma to the common Indian. But, to us children, he was above all simply a friend.

The ashram had its rules—strict always, often stern, sometimes harsh as well. Bapu made these rules. His word was final in how they were applied. But, to us children, again, he was never the stern disciplinarian, never the dictator. Between him and us, the only rule was friendship.

Let's take the example of the dining hall. The rule was that all the ashramites eat their meals in the community dining hall. Mealtime was signalled by the ashram bell.

In the ashram, this bell wielded an authority perhaps second only to Bapu's. It rang to mark the time for each activity, from rising in the morning, to going to sleep at night. Once, we figured that the bell rang fifty-six times a day. At mealtime, it would be rung three times. The first ringing called us to the dining hall. At the stroke of the second ringing, the dining hall doors closed. The third ringing began the prayers.

One time, I was late getting to the dining hall. Just as I was climbing the stairs, the bell rang for the second time. The dining hall doors slammed shut.

Now, what child anywhere on earth has adhered to the rules and regulations regarding meals? Just the same, a shut door now stood between me and my food.

I began imagining the scene on the other side of the door. People would be sitting on the floor in four rows. Their plates would have been filled with rice, vegetables, milk, and slices of yeast bread. My mother, working in the kitchen, would be worrying over my absence. Bapu, sitting near the door, would be looking around at everyone with a smile.

I don't remember whether it was someone else's idea or my own, but, standing at the closed door, I began to sing.

Open the gates, O Lord, open the gates of your temple.

When the poet Narsinhrao composed this prayer at the demise of his child, could he have foreseen such a use of his verse?

All was quiet in the dining hall, so my young voice carried inside. Bapu burst into laughter, and the doors swung open for Babla!

The ideal of Satyagraha* took root on the ashram prayer ground. On that ground flowered Bapu's life as a seeker of Truth.

When only the ashramites were at prayers, Bapu would take each one's problems and delve into how a seeker of Truth would resolve them. To him, Satyagraha was not only a means to fight the British government. It encompassed one's entire way of life. So, all facets of life were tested on the prayer ground on the anvil of the seeker of Truth.

Why is someone a late riser? Why does someone doze off during prayers? Why does someone ejaculate in his sleep? Is it hard to conquer the disease of anger? Does an ashramite need jewelry? How does diet affect the mind?

The prayer ground—how pleasing the site was. On one side was Bapu's cottage, on the other was an ancient shrine to the holy sage Dattatreya. On the third side was the Sabarmati River—most of its bed dry in the summer, roaring with flood waters during the rains, yet all year round washing the bank by the prayer ground.

Bapu used to sit under the tree on the north side. Facing Bapu, the men would sit on one side, the women on the

---

*Literally, "Truth-force." Gandhi's name for his form of active nonviolence. One who practices Satyagraha is a *Satyagrahi.*

other. When I began attending prayers, I found my place right away. I fixed myself in Bapu's lap.

When I think of it today, I realize what a privilege it was and what a responsibility it gave me. But, at the time, I knew only that Bapu's lap was the center of the prayer assembly, of the ashram, of our entire world.

After some time, I had a competitor. A friend of mine, Prabodh Choksi, came to stay in the ashram for a few days, and he too began coming to the prayer meetings to sit in Bapu's lap. Before this, I had been the youngest. But this boy was younger still and so couldn't be denied the privilege.

Bapu solved the problem by sharing his knees between us. But, after a few days, we were promoted and told to sit quietly among the others.

Small children were allowed to sit with either sex. Sometimes in the male section, we ashram boys would choose someone special and focus all our skill on imitating him. At times on the female side, we would achieve supreme satisfaction from tying the braids of women trying to commune with the Almighty.

Could anything happen in the ashram without Bapu hearing of it? Our mischief just begged to be reported.

"Bapu, the boys are harassing us at prayer time!"

We figured, now we'll be put on trial. We'll need a lawyer to plead for us, and witnesses. Or should we just boldly confess our offense like the civil disobedience people?

But we needn't have been concerned. Without even questioning us, Bapu ruled, "How could our prayers keep the children's interest? Arrange a separate program for them."

Hurray!

In a way, Bapu liked our child's play. In fact, when he had the chance, he would often play a little with us. But other times he would meet our mischief with some training device designed to discourage it. This would often prove effective.

One frequent device was to assign a late riser the ringing of the morning wake-up bell. In a similar way, he would give each of us some responsibility, to curb our exuberance and our pranks.

The job of guiding an American woman around the ashram was once given to me by Bapu. He knew that, once assigned a task, I would acquit myself faultlessly.

I led the woman around the entire ashram. With the help of her interpreter, I explained everything as best I could. In one of the cottages, she was amazed to see a grinding wheel.* She had never seen anything like it. I was more amazed at her than she was to see the stones.

I rotated the top stone, showing her how it worked. She was simply charmed. She immediately took my picture.

When we moved on, she tried to tip me with a small coin. I wouldn't take it. She coaxed me to accept. I firmly refused. Then the interpreter told me she was offering it because she was pleased to do so. So there was no harm in taking it.

---

*A set of grinding stones, one rotating on top of the other, commonly used in Indian households to hand-grind flour.

I told the interpreter, "I didn't show her around for money. I did it because Bapu told me to. If she wants to give money, she can give it to the ashram manager. I won't touch it."

In this precept of social ethics, I do not remember having been coached. I learned it from the self-respect generated from Bapu having entrusted to me the job of guide.

But I can't claim I was never tainted by corruption.

C.I.D.* agents often came to the ashram. One of them was Ismailbhai. He was heavy, dark, and wore a fez. We children were very fond of him. He used to succeed in bribing us.

I don't know whether that was his only interest, or whether he genuinely cared for us, as well. But, whenever he came, he would always bring sweets. In return, all he wanted to know was, "And what is Gandhiji up to, nowadays?"

Having sweetened our tongues with Ismailbhai's gifts, we wouldn't hesitate to leak some information. "Nowadays, Bapu is experimenting with spreads made from bitter neem leaves!"**

And the simple man would diligently write that down.

On the one hand, Bapu—scientist of Truth that he was —really was as interested in experiments with neem spread as he would be in the solution of any social or political

_____

*Central Intelligence Department, the intelligence agency of the British rulers.

**Neem is a common tree of India. Gandhi hoped to introduce its bitter but nutritious leaves into the Indian diet, to alleviate hunger and malnutrition among India's poor.

problem. On the other hand, this poor representative of the British government seriously believed that a recipe for neem spread was as important to note as a secret meeting!

But, then, who knew which of Bapu's formulas, which experiment would prove powerful enough to shake the foundations of British rule? Who could know that gathering a pinch of salt would send tremors through the Delhi throne?*

I once had a personal taste of Bapu's style of fighting.

One time, a friend of our family sent some toys for me from Bombay. There were plenty of places to play in the ashram, but few toys. So we ashram children were always happy to get them.

But, to our misfortune, the toys sent for me were foreign-made.** So, when the toys arrived, Bapu confiscated them before they ever got to us.

Our "Secret Police" informed us that some toys had been sent from Bombay for Babla, and that Bapu had hidden them. We prepared to take up arms against this gross injustice. To launch our struggle, we decided to send a deputation to Bapu. Since the toys had come in my name, I was selected the spokesman.

Our delegation arrived at Bapu's cottage. My father was sitting as usual at Bapu's side, writing. Other ashramites were there, as well.

I fired the first volley.

"Is it true that some toys have come from Bombay?"

_____

*A reference to Gandhi's Salt March.

**Gandhi was leading a national boycott of foreign goods to stop the flow of India's wealth to industrial nations.

It helps to extract a confession of fact from the opponent before the war commences in earnest.

Bapu was just then busy writing. But he looked up from his work and said, "Oh, it's you, Babla. Yes, it's true about the toys."

"Where did you put my toys?"

In the second volley was the inquiry into the whereabouts of the goods.

"They're over there on the shelf," said Bapu, pointing. The goods were not hidden at all. And there was a whole basketful of them!

"Hand over those toys!"

When justice is on your side, why beat around the bush?

But then Bapu began to set out his own argument. "You know the toys are foreign-made, don't you?"

If Bapu himself had set up the boycott of foreign goods, how could ashram children play with foreign-made toys? That was Bapu's line of reasoning. But, at our age, how could we understand such things?

"I know nothing about Indian or foreign. I only know they're my toys, and they've been sent here for me. So you have to let me have them."

I asserted my rights. I was sure Bapu would not deny me my rights.

But suddenly Bapu gave the argument a new twist.

"Can we play with foreign-made toys?"

In that word "we," Bapu played his trump card. In just one sentence, Bapu had placed me and him on the same side of the fence. As I was losing my right to play with those toys, Bapu was giving up his own. And, the moment I was shown that my opponent had shared that right, the responsibility he had taken on became mine also.

Where did our arguments vanish? Where could our delegation make its stand? When the enemy himself sides with you, the contest is completely unbalanced.

"We have ourselves launched the boycott of foreign goods, and, if we play with foreign goods here at home..."

But Bapu didn't have to pursue the argument. Seeing their spokesman unnerved, the other members of the delegation were already slipping away.

The noted child psychologist A. S. Neill once said that love can be defined as "taking sides." Even by that rough analogy, Bapu often showed his love for us.

That there was a school in the ashram was unknown to us until Miss Premaben Kantak came to teach us. On her arrival, we became aware of the school.

She was zealous as a teacher. In fact, it was almost impossible to escape her. Today I associate Premaben with the meaning of her first name—"love." But in those days we thought her surname—"thorns"—was more appropriate.

When Bapu later began promoting handcrafts as a basis for education, one teacher was reported as saying, "I already combine the use of the hands with learning. When the children get out of control, I use the cane in my hand and teach them a good lesson!"

Premaben must have been trained in this concept of education. Once we were placed in her hands, she made liberal use of them to expand our horizons of knowledge.

Like Premaben, we too were determined—determined to get away from her. Under one pretext or another, we would play hooky from the class or workshop.

If we were caught, Premaben had various ways of punishing us. One of these was making us skip a meal. But, in the domain of Bapu, master of fasting, missing a meal didn't mean much. Besides, we would offset the punishment by gorging ourselves on tomatoes and other vegetables from the ashram fields.

An instance of playing hooky. It had rained. Of all the Indian seasons, it is only the season of monsoon rains that announces its arrival with a bang. Potholes and streamlets had appeared all over the ashram.

On this morning, I had set out from home for the school. But on my way I noticed a rain-filled pothole beneath a small tree and observed that ants were drowning in it.

The savior in me was awakened. Instead of going on to class, I decided to save the ants. I took a leaf from the tree, lifted one ant out of the water with it, and brought the ant ashore.

Why only one ant? Not exactly what you'd call a mass rescue operation! But I did mean to save all the ants. Only, I intended to save them one at a time. That way, all the ants would be saved from drowning, while Babla the savior too would be saved—from drowning in the waters of the school.

But Premaben wasn't the kind to be gotten around so easily. She insisted on 100% class attendance. To ensure it, she would make a round of the entire ashram.

While I was engrossed in rescuing the ants, she came up from behind the tree and grabbed hold of my ear. Under those conditions, it would not have been wise to start a tug-of-war. Without a word, I meekly followed along. She must have fallen in love with my ear, because she wouldn't let go of it until we reached the classroom.

Bapu wasn't in the ashram just then. So I wrote him a letter. Or rather, I dictated it—because our correspondence with Bapu started long before I could write. Once a week, Pandit Khare would write down the letters to Bapu we dictated.

By this arrangement, I related to Bapu the incident of the tree and the ants and lodged a complaint about the treatment given to my ear. I also asked him, with his belief in nonviolence, how violence could be used at any time in his ashram.

There is room for differing opinions on justification in this incident. Possibly Premaben remembers it differently than I do. But what is certain is that Bapu was on our side in our fight against the grownups.

After a few days, Premaben received a letter from Bapu. I don't know what was in it. But I do know that at that point her experiment in thrashing was abandoned.

If Gandhiji was *Bapu*—"Father"—then what did I call my own father?* I called him "Uncle."

During my childhood, Bapu and Uncle were both like guests passing through our home. Of course, Sabarmati Ashram was their base. But when did they ever spend much

*Mahadev Desai, Gandhi's chief secretary from 1917 to 1942.

time there? They were either traveling around the country, or in prison.

My entire childhood seems to me an alternation between the periods when the grownups were in prison and the brief periods they were free. When Uncle came home from a time in prison, while Mother was busy preparing some tasty dishes, I would ask him, "When are you going back?"

Uncle would burst into laughter and say, "Whenever the government again chooses to make me its guest and whisks me away."

For the people of India, this period in the freedom struggle was a formative one. For the first time, reputable citizens looked on imprisonment as a badge of honor, on prison itself as a palace.

As for us ashram children, we were used to the government's hospitable invitations. Once when the black police van came to pick up Uncle, I said to him, "Why do you get such short prison terms? This time get a longer one!"

And now my memories revolve around the prison visit. Cut-off pants and short-sleeved shirt, striped blue. Normally, Uncle looked smart in any style of dress. But the prison uniform demeaned him.

He would talk to Mother about household matters. But all my questions would be about the world inside the prison. The barracks, the food, the work, his fellow prisoners—the stories he told about these came from a land that was to me completely alien.

In the freedom struggle, imprisonment played several indirect roles, along with its central one. For one thing, it conquered people's fear of the government. Imprisonment itself was no longer seen as a dire threat. Second, prison life toughened those in the movement, preparing them for later rigors. Third, prison became a university for self-directed study.

Each of these aspects came into play during Uncle's time in the Hindulga Central Prison.*

All his prison terms affected our family. But this time the police went to our home village to try to collect Uncle's fine. The way my grandmother Ichhaben stood up to the policemen's insults and refused payment showed how the movement had bred fearlessness even among those in remote villages.

Uncle suffered greatly in this prison term. This was mostly due to loneliness, especially while in solitary confinement. For a long time, none of us were allowed to visit him. After that, correspondence with Mother and me was banned, because the warden could not read Gujarati, the native language of our province, and neither Mother nor I knew English.

After many months, when we finally got to see him, his looks had changed. The few hairs on his balding head had turned gray. There were wrinkles on his face. He had lost a few teeth. He showed all the signs of old age.

He was being kept apart from his fellow political prisoners. The ordinary prisoners were not allowed to talk with him. But Uncle had a word of praise for a Muslim prisoner who had wordlessly shown his affection by taking on some of Uncle's labor.

---

*In what is now Karnataka state.

During this imprisonment, Uncle did an English translation of Bapu's *The Yoga of Selfless Action*. He also wrote
a treatise on the Gita.* Apart from his journals, this book
may be his best.

The prison took away Uncle's youth, but it also gave
him the Gita.

At the time of Bapu's Salt March, I was barely six. But
the entire ashram in those days was going through a political awakening. So, at an age when other children could
scarcely begin to understand, we knew well the meanings
of prison, police, C.I.D., court.

The songs we heard in the ashram ran: *Don't kill,
learn to die—this is what Gandhiji teaches. Think of prison as a temple, and you will be free.* Mixed with such
songs were others saying, *The spinning wheel is an arrow
that will pierce the government's heart. Victory to the
revolution.* And, *Oh, you with the hat, how did you come
to our land?*

As for myself, my impression is that I may have
harbored anger towards some unseen power called the
government, but none towards any of its representatives—
light or dark, high or low. On the contrary, we were
friendly with people like Ismailbhai and others we came in
contact with. For this attitude, Bapu's own approach was as
much or maybe more responsible than our own childlike
nature.

---

*The Bhagavad Gita, holiest of Hindu books and part of the great
national epic, the Mahabharata. Mahadev Desai's book was later published as *The Gita According to Gandhi*.

On March 12, 1930, Bapu announced that he would march to Dandi and there break the law by collecting salt from the beach.*

In the ashram, it was presumed that Bapu would be arrested before he could set out. But, as the day approached, everyone in the ashram was eager to go with Bapu on the march. When Bapu announced his selection, the chosen seventy-nine were joyful. We children were indignant at being left out.

On the eve of the march, the prayer ground proved too small for the multitudes assembled. The congregation had to be moved to the vast dry bed of the Sabarmati. The roaring voice of Pandit Khare, who led our hymns, proved too weak to reach such crowds.

People continued to gather through the night—hundreds of thousands of them. Beneath the ashram's ancient tamarind tree were parked what seemed like all the cars then in Ahmedabad.

Pandit Khare, surrounded by the crowd, could not reach the prayer ground. So from where he stood he began the hymn *Raghupati Raghav Rajaram*—"Rama, heir of Ragu, is the great Master." I believe it was from this time on that this hymn became known as the Gandhian hymn.

---

*The British government had legislated themselves a monopoly on salt production in order to secure revenue from a tax on salt. Gandhi saw this tax as particularly evil, since it affected even the poorest of the poor. At the same time, defiance of the salt laws symbolically represented opposition to all of British rule.

Gandhi's plan—at first thought harmless by many—proved a master stroke, setting a fire under the Indian public and leading to countless acts of opposition to British rule around the country.

Hundreds of thousands waited to see Gandhiji begin his march. But, after prayers, Bapu visited the sick. Three children had recently died of smallpox. One of them was Pandit Khare's son. Yet Panditji was at the head of the march.

At the sight of the marchers, our teacher Premaben was mad with joy. She clipped a badge on Bapu's shawl and embraced him. Another woman of the ashram placed the traditional dot of red paste on his forehead. Garlands of homespun yarn were slipped over the heads of the marchers.

To the strains of *Vaishnav Jan*—"Vishnu's Devotee" —and the chanting of Rama's name, Bapu set out. The entire city of Ahmedabad walked with him to the next village to give the marchers a send-off.

We children were left behind in the ashram. After Bapu started off, we raised our flags and began our march—in the opposite direction—straight to the gates of Sabarmati Prison.

We were not going to be left out!

In Sabarmati village, across from the liquor shop that stood behind the prison, the ashram women stood in vigil, singing of the evils of drink. Newspaper reporters and others had gathered to find out what the women were up to and what would happen to them. Catching hold of one of the women's hands, I too had joined the chorus: *Drinking has destroyed everything, oh addict. Give it up!*

A new chapter in the freedom struggle was opening before my young eyes.

People had doubts about this new tack of Bapu's. But, in the days following Bapu's Salt March, the women were full of a fearlessness Bapu had generated in them.*

Perhaps this was his finest initiative in this period following the Salt March. The involvement of women was a new wave in the life of the country. The national prohibition campaign itself was restricted to women. This move of Bapu's reserved a special place of pride for women throughout India.

In these days, the ashram hummed with constant activity. Fresh news of actions around the country continued to pour in. Uncle was addressing public meetings in Ahmedabad, where the audiences ran into the hundreds of thousands.

In the Gujarati city of Borsad, women organized a procession to protest government policies, in defiance of government orders. Women from the ashram took part in this. Led by old Gangaben, they braved police batons with smiles on their lips. Gangaben's white homespun sari turned pink with the blood drawn by a baton blow to her head.

---

*Women all over India picketed liquor shops in the prohibition campaign launched by Gandhi in the days following the Salt March. Gandhi felt that the liquor trade, benefiting the British rulers with its tax revenue, seriously hurt India by drawing the hopeless poor into even more hopeless drinking.

Previous to this, many Indian women were not even allowed in public—so Gandhi's call to the women was both revolutionary and liberating. Though Gandhi is rightly criticized for his treatment of his wife in their early years of marriage, he is considered in India to be that country's greatest champion of women's rights. The degree of freedom and equality enjoyed by women in Gandhi's ashrams was almost unknown in India at the time.

Bapu was released from prison and for a short while returned to the ashram. In his sacred fire, Bapu was always offering one sacrifice after another.

One day, he called a meeting of the few women still in the ashram. We children were not allowed in, but we heard about it later. Bapu had asked these remaining women to court imprisonment. This included mothers, like mine.

Bapu's call was the call of the nation, the call of abused humankind. There was no question of denying it. But this would be the first time both Uncle and Mother would be in prison. I wasn't the only one troubled by that. Mother and Uncle too were perplexed.

Anasuyaben Sarabhai* had offered to put up all the ashram children at her Harijan Hostel. But Uncle and Mother wanted to make special arrangements for me. So I went with two other children to stay with another friend of the ashram's, where our studies would be well looked after.

But, even though this friend's house had more to offer us, we were not prepared to stay separate from the other ashram children. We stayed there for one night. But I cried all night.

We were then moved to Anasuyaben's hostel. But, despite all Anasuyaben's affection, the hostel was not well equipped to handle us.

Bapu returned to prison with a historic vow: "I would rather die like a dog or crow than return to the ashram before India is free." And why should the ashram remain untouched while the government confiscated the land of

*Anasuya Sarabhai was a benefactor and associate of Gandhi's. Her hostel was an institution for the welfare of "untouchables."

farmers? So he wrote to the government, voluntarily sur-
rendering to it all the ashram buildings and grounds.

Most of the ashramites, male and female, wound up in
prison. The rest returned to their home provinces to work
there for the movement. The ashram turned desolate.

One time, we went back from Anasuyaben's place to
see the ashram. The sight brought tears to our eyes.

Once full of our games and songs, the ashram now
bore a stoney silence. The ashram buildings looked fright-
ful. Some were missing a door or window. The grounds,
once faultlessly groomed, were covered by tall weeds,
which had already withered. Worst of all, Bapu was absent.

We didn't feel like staying long. But, for a little while,
we sat beneath the ancient tamarind tree.

It was the biggest tree in the ashram, and had been
there long before the ashram was built. It had sheltered the
tents of Bapu and the others when they first arrived. It had
seen the ashram buildings gradually rise up. The black jail
van had stopped beneath it many times. Many times, too,
the limousines of the Ahmedabad rich had parked there.
Beneath this tree, not so long before, the ashramites had
taken leave of Bapu as he started his march to the sea.

For a while we sat there, wordless, feeling that the
tamarind too must be sighing.

2

Sevagram Ashram

For years, we three had not lived together as a family. Uncle would either be in prison or on tour. In 1932, Mother too had been jailed. So we had been torn asunder.

When Bapu moved from Wardha to Segaon, Uncle stayed behind at Maganwadi to handle the mail and to look after guests arriving in the city. Figuring that things would soon settle down, Uncle brought us from Sabarmati to Wardha.

It was at this time that Bapu chose a path that would prove arduous and painful. He turned his steps toward the villages.

What kind of villages had captured Bapu's attention? In the villages that held Bapu's concern, none had the strength to raise their heads against poverty. Filth and disease had numbed the people.

At the beginning of his stay at Maganwadi, Bapu had begun going to clean an adjoining village. This was no jungle hamlet far from the railroad track, but a village right by the city of Wardha! By the time I came to Maganwadi, Bapu had moved to Segaon. But my father had started going to the village in his place.*

For months on end, the villagers looked on Bapu, Mahadevbhai, and their companions, as ordinary sweepers. Only, these were better, because they took no money for their work!

"Go over there. It's dirtier on that side." So said one who had just relieved himself, pointing to the spot he had soiled.

In Sabarmati Ashram, I too had taken my turn at emptying toilets. But this only meant to dump the buckets of "night soil" into compost pits and to scrub the buckets with a coconut-leaf broom.

Here, fresh feces had to be lifted directly with a tin dustpan. And when the feces were stale, they were full of worms. My father diligently collected all of it.

Once, at Segaon, I asked Bapu, "What good is this work? It doesn't affect the people. In fact, they just point to other places they've soiled, and tell us to clean over there."

Bapu said, "Is that all that's bothering you? Are you so easily discouraged? Ask Mahadev how long he's been at it. There is devotion in his work. You too must acquire this spirit. The bane of untouchability is no ordinary blemish on

*Gandhi and Desai were cleaning feces from the streets and yards, where people normally relieved themselves. This work was to encourage the villagers to adopt better habits of sanitation. It was also to break down the taboo against proper Hindus disposing of their own feces. This taboo had created and sustained the need for a class of "untouchables," social outcasts who could perform this work because it would not further defile them.

our society. We will have to perform a prolonged penance to remove it."

I was not so easily convinced. "But, Bapu, what's the good of it, if they don't improve?"

Bapu took a new tack. "Why, it's good for the person sweeping, isn't it? It's good training."

"But the villagers too need that training."

Bapu smiled and said, "I see you are a lawyer. But there is truth in what you say. If we knew how to train them in this, I would dance for joy."

Pursuing his thoughts further, he said, "If I was in your place, I would keep careful watch. When I saw someone getting up from his squat, I would approach him and say politely, 'Friend, you are having bowel problems. You must take such and such steps to remedy it.' In this way, I would win his heart."

My silence would only feed Bapu's enthusiasm. "If I had my way, I would be out there sweeping those roads myself. Not only that, I would plant flowers there and water them daily. Where there are dung heaps today, I would make gardens. Sweeping is an art in itself!"

He had himself started to work in Segaon village. At the same time, he had begun setting up institutions to handle various aspects of village development nationwide. The headquarters of each of these organizations served in part as a research center.

The All-India Village Industries Association was headquartered at Maganwadi. In one area, we were running bullock-powered oil presses; in another, paper was made by hand. Bapu would lose himself in experiments with different kinds of grinding stones. Experiments with bitter neem and tamarind spreads were ongoing.

Bapu wanted to find out what kind of hearth used the least wood in cooking. Experiments were carried out to develop lanterns that could run on food oil. Experiments were also carried out on production methods for raw sugar, date juice, and much else.

When Bapu focussed on village life, each of his activities revolved around just one consideration: Will the hungry receive succor from it? Just as the strings of an instrument resonate to a singer's voice, Bapu's heartstrings would reverberate with the slightest cry of agony from the hungry, the needy.

Traveling by train with Bapu was an enriching experience. At that time, Bapu traveled in ordinary third-class cars. Only later did necessity force him to use cars specially hooked up for him. Of course, even in the ordinary cars, people would at once move aside and make room for him.

Bapu's retinue was not exactly small. Ashramites, patients, guests, research workers—all were part of the herd. Nor was there much attention to the maxim, "Travel light." Baggage was always heavy.

This baggage was in the charge of Kanubhai,* with me as his helper. It was our job to move it on and off the train. People would leave their bags with us before boarding and give them no further thought until they ran to us for them after leaving the train. We had developed a routine to

---

*Kanu Gandhi, a young relative of Gandhi's. His camera helped document Gandhi's later years.

transport the baggage, shove it onto the train, organize it, and take it off. The bags would be counted once, twice, three times.

But, because of the confusion around Bapu, the orderliness of our procedure could never be strictly maintained. For instance, those who joined us part way through would add their bags to the load and not bother to inform us. Once, to find the baggage of such a person, Kanubhai was forced to extend his train trip by many stations.

But we didn't really mind any of this, as long as Kasturba was there to assure us of our "coolie charge." That was our name for snacks we received during the journey or at its end. Both Kanubhai and his assistant were brisk in carrying the baggage, as also in consuming the coolie charge.

The far corner seat was saved for Bapu. We took the platform sleeping berths above the seats. But once I was scolded by Kanubhai and Uncle for spreading my bedding on the berth above Bapu's seat. According to our travel code, no one slept in this berth, out of respect for Bapu.

Most of the time Bapu would stay sitting by the window. Once in a while he would use a berth to stretch out on. But it was hard for Bapu to rest on the way. Any hour of the day or night, at station after station, large or small, the crowds would allow him no rest.

As the train pulled into the station, we would hear shouts of *Mahatma Gandhi ki jai!*— "Victory to Mahatma Gandhi!" The same cry would echo as the train pulled out.

The period I'm now writing about—1936 to 1940— could be seen as a low point in India's freedom struggle.

But there was never an ebb in the numbers wanting to pay their respects to Bapu.

At night, we used to cover the compartment's ceiling light with a special blue cloth cover, so Bapu could sleep awhile. But people would shine flashlights in his face through the windows. We would pull down the shutters. Then people would smash the windows in the compartment lavatory. At one station on the way to Delhi from Wardha, these windows were smashed both on our way and on our return.

Sometimes Uncle would plead with the people: "Gandhiji is sleeping now. Won't you keep quiet?" People would answer, "He is a god. He needs no sleep."

Such an argument would enrage Uncle. "The gods you know are the ones you see in the temple. This god has to move around. He works for your sake, day and night. Won't you let him rest?"

At many stops during the daylight hours, snacks, baskets of fruit, even full meals, would reach us from the crowd. The hungry eyes of Kanubhai and his assistant would watch for the "coolie charge."

But Bapu's own hungry eyes would be elsewhere. At each station, without fail, he would collect money for the Harijan* Fund. I believe this practice began in 1934, when he toured the country on behalf of the Harijans, and it continued till the end. Bapu would stretch his hands out the window, and they would at once be full of money. We too would put out our hands or kerchiefs.

---

*Literally, "Child of God." This was the new name Gandhi gave to the untouchables, to help remove their stigma. Social and economic uplift of Harijans was one of Gandhi's main causes.

I couldn't understand why people gave away money to others. But we would see that all our palms were full. At times, we would reach the next station before we could finish counting the coins from the station before.

Many times, I thought, "Do these people know why Bapu asks for their money? When they get home, will they give up the practice of untouchability? Will the Harijans' condition improve by this giving?"

But, in the eyes of those who gave, I could see faith. All they came for was to pay their respects to the Mahatma. Along with that, they offered some money. Of course, they must have heard the phrase, "Harijan Fund." Some of them must have known its meaning.

But I came to realize that these people with their faith knew only one thing perfectly: No matter how busy Bapu was, he never forgot the poor.

It was true. For instance, many times the train would halt at a station, and Bapu would be busy writing. Bapu's writing would go on, but his other hand would be stretched out the window. At those times, he would not even ask for money. Yet his palm would be full of coins.

The Indian public worshipped one who cared for the poor. On seeing this poverty incarnate, the poorest of the poor turned donor. Through all the slavery, poverty, and ignorance of centuries, it was such faith that had sustained the spirit of the common people.

In the twenty-five years Uncle was with Bapu, Uncle took off from work twice. These were the two times he was sick. The first time, he was bedridden with typhoid. The second time, it was high blood pressure. He took an official leave and went to Simla for a rest. In his next illness, he took permanent leave, and passed away.

In twenty-five years, he took no other time off—no Sunday, no holiday, no summer vacation. Even when his father died, Uncle kept up his work.

It was in 1938, at Maganwadi, that his blood pressure shot up. At times, he would get dizzy. The obvious cause was that, each day, he had to walk from Wardha to Sevagram and back again, in the Wardha heat. Some days he had to walk it twice—twenty-two miles altogether. Wardha's summer temperatures ranged between 115 and 120 degrees.

Only Uncle could have taken on the burden of Bapu's assignments on top of such physical strain. For ten or fifteen years, I had watched Uncle work at least fifteen hours each day. When we moved from Maganwadi to Sevagram, the walking ended, but work hours correspondingly increased.

Uncle's work entailed going through Bapu's mail, writing some replies, dealing with people who had come to talk with Bapu, taking notes of important discussions and meetings, and writing or translating articles for the *Harijan* weeklies.* Besides these standard assignments, he might be preparing a book, writing articles for dailies, or addressing public gatherings.

Work with Bapu was an extraordinarily heavy load. What was amazing was how well Uncle coped with it. The key to this feat was the complete identification he had

---

*Gandhi's journals, one in Hindi, one in English.

developed with Bapu. In this relationship was a rare fusion of devotion to a superior and allegiance to a colleague.

In Ahmedabad in 1915, when Uncle had first gone to meet Bapu, Bapu had looked through the writings Uncle showed him and said, "Your place is beside me." On his way home from that same meeting, Uncle had told a friend, "If I were to spend my entire life at the feet of one person, it would be this one." It was this love at first sight that gradually matured into a complete identification.

Uncle had an independent personality completely different from Bapu's. Bapu's genius was strong like the sun. Uncle's was mild like the moon. Bapu's devotion was to his work. Uncle was devoted to a person. Bapu towered and shone like the Himalayas. Uncle had compassion as wide as the river Ganga.

Yet, despite these differences, the degree of psychic unity between the two was astonishing.

In writing, Bapu was pragmatic, a master of brevity. If one word served his purpose, he would use no more. Uncle, on the other hand, would fly in fits of fancy. His personal writings were lavishly lyrical, full of lovely figures of speech.

And yet Uncle in his articles had mastered Bapu's style. Readers of the *Harijan* weeklies would often comment that, without the initials at the end of the articles, they wouldn't know whether the author was M.D. —Mahadev Desai— or M.K.G. —Mohandas K. Gandhi.

Whatever articles Uncle wrote for the weeklies would always first go to Bapu for approval. Bapu would go through them carefully and correct them if needed. But many times Bapu would find an article so close to his own thinking, he would initial the article himself, and it would be published as his.

To save Bapu's time, national leaders—sometimes even Jawaharlal Nehru—would talk things over with Uncle and be done with it.

Not that everyone understood this special identification. Once a Punjabi gentleman wanted an appointment with Bapu. After discussing the man's business with him, Uncle told him, "Now you don't need to see Bapu."

But the man wasn't satisfied. He left, came back, talked to Uncle again, and left again. As he left the second time, he told an ashramite, "I am surely going to shoot Mahadevbhai." On hearing this, Mother was a little alarmed. But Uncle only laughed.

Uncle did not know shorthand. But his speed in writing things down was extraordinary. He would shorten some words. But he would not miss one word of Bapu's.

A few Americans once came to talk with Bapu. Uncle was taking notes as usual. A woman from the American group was also taking notes, in shorthand. The next day, she and Uncle compared notes. She was astounded.

"You beat me hands down," she said.

But simple speed in transcription was not all that was required of Uncle in taking notes of Bapu.

Bapu's speeches were always delivered impromptu, and they were not always organized or coherent. There was a naturalness, but no order. Uncle would organize the speech as he wrote it down. At one important national conference, as Bapu gave his speech impromptu in Hindi,

Uncle wrote a re-ordered English translation directly onto a telegram form, for dispatch worldwide immediately after.

Sometimes even Bapu's colleagues couldn't figure out what Bapu had said. But they would comfort themselves, saying, "We will know when we get Mahadevbhai's notes."

I once witnessed a remarkable example of the psychic unison between Bapu and Uncle. The two were standing in front of Bapu's cottage, talking. Suddenly Bapu said, "Mahadev, take this down." Bapu began dictating, and Uncle, still standing, started writing.

I was standing beside the two and watching. After awhile, I noticed that Uncle's writing had pulled ahead of Bapu's dictation. Before Bapu could say what he wanted to, Uncle would figure out what it was, and write it down.

But, at one point, Bapu dictated a word different from what Uncle had set down. So Uncle interrupted him.

"Bapu, wait, I've written a different word here. Why did you use this other word instead?"

Bapu was somewhat amused. But he too was particular about words.

"Mahadev, how could you use this other word? I would never use any word but the one I dictated."

There followed a discussion on which word was more appropriate in Bapu's usage. That took more time than the actual dictation. In the end, the word that was kept was the one Bapu spoke—but only after Bapu conceded that the word Mahadev had written was also correct.

Uncle once described Sevagram Ashram as Gandhiji's menagerie. Bapu was always surrounded by strange people.

At times, Sardar* would get irritated at some of them. Then Uncle would tell him, "Bapu is a doctor. And doctors are always surrounded by patients, aren't they?"

I have no desire to describe all the peculiarities of the ashram men. Nor could I do so.

In Sabarmati Ashram, there was one person who at each dinner would eat exactly fifty-five chappatis.** If by mistake he was served fifty-four, he would shout, "How stingy! Do you want to starve me to death?" If by accident he was given fifty-six, he would yell, "Do you take me for a ravening demon?" In this way he walked a thin line between starvation and demonhood.

In Sevagram, there was another gentleman, with whom I had the following dialog:

"Well, what are you experimenting on nowadays?" (My question.)

"Oh, there's always one thing or other. Right now, it's water."

"Do you mean you're drinking boiled water? Or trying a water therapy?"

"No, nothing to do with food or health. This time it is toilet water."

"What do you mean?"

"I mean, how to use the least water to flush the toilet."

"Oh, really?"

"Yes. Progressively reducing the amount, I now have it down to two ounces. Many areas of the country are

---

*Sardar Vallabhbhai Patel, a political colleague of Bapu, and a leading figure in the freedom struggle.

**Flat wheat cakes. A staple in the meals of north India.

suffering a severe water shortage. If we could save some water here..."

Of course, he did not explain how saving water in Wardha would help areas of the country where water was short.

Yet these ashramites with their idiosyncracies had no dearth of valuable experience. To be around some of them was a rare privilege.

One I think of in particular is Acharya Bhansali—our Uncle Bhansali. A fifty-five day fast at Sabarmati Ashram had somehow unhinged his mind. On his way by foot from the ashram to the Himalayas, he decided to observe silence for twelve years.

After a long trek through the mountains, he returned to the plains. One night, he was given a place to sleep in a cattle shed. Wakened by the sound of the cattle moving about in the night, Uncle Bhansali shouted out, "Who's there?"

He at once realized he had broken his vow of silence. From then on, he had on his mind a method to insure his vow even in sleep. He had hit upon the method right away. But he had to go a long way before finding a goldsmith willing to apply it.

The goldsmith took a copper wire, heated it red hot, and stitched together Uncle Bhansali's lips.

The same technician made him a tube that could be inserted into his mouth at one end and into which liquid could be poured. At that time, Uncle Bhansali was on a diet of raw flour and bitter neem leaves. The flour would now be made into a paste and sucked through the tube. The neem leaves could still be pushed into his mouth from one end.

When Uncle Bhansali reached Sevagram Ashram, Bapu ordered the wire removed.

But Uncle Bhansali was still sticking to his vow of twelve years' silence. Then Bapu argued him into making an exception of saying the name of God.

The debate between Bapu and Uncle Bhansali continued. Bapu would speak and Uncle Bhansali would scribble. Then Bapu persuaded him to break his silence for the purpose of the discussions. In time, he persuaded Uncle Bhansali to break his silence also in order to teach.*

However much Uncle Bhansali would have liked to insist on something, he would not argue with Bapu if Bapu said no. Only once have I seen him maintain a stand against Bapu. Bapu had advised an ashram woman to leave because of a minor lapse on her part. She was a widow.

Uncle Bhansali thought Bapu was being unjust. He told Bapu, "If she leaves, then I'm leaving too." Bapu backed down.

Uncle Bhansali would be deeply moved by the sufferings of the poor and weak. The mass rape of some women in Ashti-Chimur by British soldiers stirred him to the core. The resulting fast is an unforgettable chapter in Indian history. He spent the first fifteen days of the fast on foot. During that time, he abstained even from water. For the next forty-eight days, he was bedridden.

Day followed day. The public, numbed by British repression of the 1942 uprisings, stirred afresh. The government didn't know how to deal with the moral weapon of fasting, wielded on an issue of pure morality, by someone

*Originally, Bhansali had been a French teacher.

of saintly character. In the end, with government assurance of an inquiry, Uncle Bhansali secured the honor of Indian womanhood.

If Sevagram was a menagerie, Uncle Bhansali was its lion — striding in all splendor.

The role of the "better half" in the lives of great men would make an interesting study. Just like many other such wives, Ba* played a significant role in the career of her husband.

But her role had its special features too. At the beginning of her adult life, she was a simple, illiterate wife. But, at the time of her death, Bapu said of her, "She was the Universal Mother."

How did someone seemingly so ordinary cover such a distance in her lifetime? Of course, marriage to someone like Mahatma Gandhi is not everyone's opportunity. And Kasturba's own progress came mostly from being joined to one who was in all ways progressive. But marriage alone was not the reason. In a real sense, she had become not only a wife but a colleague.

Practising religion in the company of the Mahatma was no ordinary matter. As Uncle put it, it was like sitting on top of a volcano. Ba's complete devotion to Bapu allowed her to manage it. But in the midst of this devotion she remained an individual. At times, she even brought Bapu back on track.

---

*Literally, "Mother." This was a name commonly given to Gandhi's wife, Kasturbai. She is also called *Kasturba*—a kind of shorthand for "Mother Kasturbai."

Once, in South Africa, Ba had refused to clean the chamber pot of a Harijan clerk who worked with Bapu and lived with them. In his anger, Bapu tried to throw her out of the house. Ba cried out piteously, "Have you no shame? Where am I to go in this foreign land?"

Bapu himself used to relate this incident with tears in his eyes, as one that had opened those eyes when blinded by dogma.

After that, throughout her life, Ba kept her individuality. She shared his ordeals. Along with him, she changed her lifestyle. But all this was by her own free will.

She would join sincerely in Bapu's prayers taken from different religions. But, at the same time, she unfailingly performed her obligations as a Hindu.

The members of Bapu's extended family saw in Ba the reflection of their own mothers. But, unlike Bapu, Ba's larger family never made her care less for her own blood relations.

Her eldest son Harilal put her through the most tortuous of ordeals. From the time of his youth, Harilal had resented Bapu for denying him a formal education. He had been in revolt against Bapu ever since. After his wife died, he took to bad company and bad ways.

All this pained Ba greatly. When he embraced Islam out of spite for Bapu, Ba wrote him a pathetic letter telling of her anguish. But Harilal's reaction was, "Ba didn't write this letter. Someone else wrote it and signed her name."

All of Ba's sons were away from her. Manilal was in South Africa running *Indian Opinion*.* Ramdas was

*The journal Gandhi founded in South Africa.

supporting his family on an ordinary job in Nagpur. Devdas was the managing editor of the *Hindustan Times* newspaper. But Ba's grandchildren often stayed at Sabarmati or Sevagram, as did Bapu's nephews and nieces, and other young relations. So Ba did get the chance to exercise her maternal instincts.

Apart from these, Ba sometimes found herself taking on as her own some additional "relatives" of Bapu.

Once, a few Harijans had decided to perform Satyagraha to protest government discrimination. But their idea of Satyagraha was quite different from Bapu's. When Bapu offered Satyagraha to protest injustice, he would risk his life. These Harijans intended to fast, as Bapu often did. But there wasn't much risk in it. One person at a time would fast, each for a day!

The Harijans asked Bapu to provide space in his ashram for their "Satyagraha." Bapu told them to look around the ashram and choose any place they liked. After visiting all the buildings, they settled on Ba's cottage! This cottage had one room about 12 feet square, a verandah, and a bathroom. The Harijans selected the large room and the verandah. That left Ba the bathroom.

Bapu asked Ba, "What do you say? These people like your big room. Why don't we let them use it?"

Ba said, "They're *your* children. Give them space in *your* cottage."

With a smile, Bapu said, "Aren't my children yours too?"

Without another word, Ba vacated her room.

This "Satyagraha" lasted only a few days. When no

new "Satyagrahis" came forward as replacements, it was wound up. But, as long as it lasted, the "Satyagrahis" were in command of Ba's space. They weren't clean in their habits, either. But Ba tolerated all that. What's more, she would bring them drinking water and inquire about their health.

Once Ba had accepted them as her children, what did it matter if they were clean? Her duty was only to serve her children with love.

Usually Bapu took the job of serving meals. He would explain to the guests about his various dietary experiments: "There is a spoonful of baking soda in this baked chappati. Do you know what this spread is made of? Taste it and you'll know. The taste of neem may be bitter, but not its effect! Garlic is good for blood pressure."

Ba would help Bapu serve. But she would serve things like butter, chunks of raw sugar, and other sweets. We children were more interested in what was served by Ba than by Bapu, and she in turn most enjoyed serving us children. If a package of sweets was delivered to the ashram, she would hold it for us. Even when traveling, she would make sure we were well fed.

She never grew too old to want to learn something new. Of course, Bapu's company by itself was a great education. But I have seen many who, even after having stayed with Bapu, remained as dull as before. Not so with Ba.

Her command of language was meager. So the doors of knowledge were in that way almost closed for her. But this did not stop Ba. She approached new knowledge with a childlike eagerness.

Once, she called me to her and asked, "Babla, what are you studying nowadays?"

I told her, "English, science, geometry, carpentry, Hindi grammar, and the Ramayana."*

English and math were beyond Ba. So she said, "Could you give me lessons on the Ramayana?"

I was perplexed. I said, "Ba, you had better learn it from Ramnarayanji. He's the one teaching me. I'm just a beginner."

Ba said, "Oh, no. I don't know if he'd have the time. And anyway, I need someone who can explain it in Gujarati. I'll tell you what. Whatever you learn from him during the day, teach me in the evening. I too am a beginner!"

For the next few evenings, seventy-year-old Kasturba took lessons in the Ramayana from fifteen-year old Babla. Even now, whenever I open the pages of that book, I see before me Rama's wife Sita, mother of the world, sitting beside that other mother of the world, Kasturba—both of them pure, serene, filled with devotion.

It was when Sevagram was given a post office that we moved there from Maganwadi. A cottage was built for us, close to Bapu's. On one side was Ba's cottage, then Bapu's, then ours—a pattern symbolic of the trio, Bapu, Ba, and Mahadevbhai.

Though our cottage was so close to Bapu's, and though Uncle spent most of his time with him, Mother and I rarely visited Bapu's cottage. We two and Uncle had decided that Bapu should not be given any added strain.

*The Hindu epic story of Lord Rama, considered an incarnation of the god Vishnu.

In 1942, Uncle's work load grew heavier. Often Uncle tried to get some essential afternoon rest. Before going to his room, he would bolt the cottage door and tell me, "Babla, I'm retiring for awhile. Don't wake me up for anyone." To make doubly sure, he would add, "Even if death knocks, tell him, 'You'll have to wait. Uncle is resting, and I won't let you in.'"

I didn't want to hear about death. To change the subject, I would ask, "What if Bapu comes?"

That question would get no answer. He could never imagine resting if Bapu needed him.

Ordinarily, Uncle and Mother didn't have much time even to talk to each other. Meals were about the only time. And that too in front of everyone! It would have been hard to have kept their affairs private. In any case, there wasn't anything concerning the household they would try to keep secret from me.

For example, Uncle got only a small salary from Bapu, which was never raised. Often we had trouble managing on it. Sometimes, when we fell too far behind, Uncle would write newspaper articles to earn us some extra income. Sometimes there would be a decision to cut our expenses still further.

Uncle and Mother would include me in discussions on such matters. As a result, I too felt I had a stake in the affairs of the household. And for a few days I would make sure my shorts weren't torn while playing. I never had anything like an allowance or wanted to ask for one.

When Bapu began his talk of demanding that the British "Quit India," Uncle's work load began multiplying.

There was a spate of visitors. The correspondence pile grew higher. More articles had to be written.

To top it off, Bapu had declared, "This time in prison will be different from earlier times. This time, I intend to refuse both food and water." This further multiplied Uncle's worries. He didn't at all like the idea of Bapu's fasting as soon as he entered prison. Within the ashram, a flurry of notes passed between Uncle and Bapu.

Uncle's health was suffering. The onset of the struggle seemed just around the corner. So Bapu persuaded him to take some time off to rest.

Shri Birla* offered to take Uncle with him to the city of Nasik. It was decided he would stay there a week. Neither Mother nor I was to go with him.

Shortly after Uncle left, a phone call came from Wardha. The message was that Uncle had gotten dizzy at the railway station and so had not taken the train. Bapu sent a return message for Uncle to be brought back to Sevagram at once. But meanwhile Uncle had been taken to the hospital. I had never before seen Bapu look so worried.

It was a Sunday. Each week, Bapu would start his day of silence on Sunday evening, keeping it until the following evening. This Sunday, even after beginning his silence, he kept walking from his cottage over to the small building next to it where the phone was kept, to find out the news about Uncle. He would write notes asking about Uncle's condition.

Finally the car came, bringing Uncle. He was brought straight to our cottage. Bapu came running. Uncle was laid

---

*G. D. Birla, a benefactor of Gandhi's.

on the bed Mother had prepared. Bapu sat on the bed and took Uncle's head in his lap.

"Mahadev, how do you feel now?"

For the first time since his nephew Maganlal's death, Bapu had broken his weekly silence.

"Fine enough now. My wish is fulfilled. At the station, I thought my time was up. So I told them I didn't want to go either to Nasik or the hospital. I said, 'If this is the end, I want to go with my head in Bapu's lap.' But they took me to the hospital anyway."

Bapu kept stroking Uncle's head. A few months later, when Uncle died as a prisoner in the Aga Khan palace, his head was again in Bapu's lap.

3

The Last Struggle

Shortly after midnight of August 8, 1942, Bapu electrified the nation with a speech calling for the British government to "Quit India."* At the close of his speech, Bapu said, "I will write a final letter to the Viceroy. If I do not receive a favorable reply from him within two weeks, I will launch national resistance."

After the meeting, Bapu returned to Birla House.** He held his usual evening prayer meeting there. Then, feeling at ease, he retired to a sound sleep.

But, for two others within the house, sleep proved impossible: Uncle and Kasturba. My bed was next to Uncle's. The clock in the main room struck one.

Kasturba came in. "What time is it, Mahadev?"

"One o'clock, Ba."

---

*Feeling India could wait no longer, Gandhi and his political colleagues had decided to make a final, irrevocable demand for the British rulers to "Quit India" at once.

**The Bombay residence of Gandhi's benefactor, G. D. Birla. A more famous Birla House is in New Delhi.

"What do you think? Will they arrest Bapu tonight?"

"I think they will. I don't see how they can let him remain free after his speech this evening. But Bapu doesn't think they'll arrest him for at least these two weeks. Often what Bapu thinks doesn't seem reasonable, but turns out to be true anyway. So, who knows?"

I was by turns dozing off, and waking to the chiming of the clock. Two o'clock. Three o'clock. Four o'clock.

At four o'clock, Uncle said, "Bapu may have been right, after all. The Bombay police usually come like thieves in the night to make their arrests. It's coming on dawn, now, so maybe they don't plan to arrest him yet. But they must have arrested Sardar. His speech yesterday was too scathing for them to leave him free for a minute. Let's phone over to where he's staying, and find out."

The phone didn't work. The line had been cut. One of us left to use a neighbor's phone. But he returned from the gate and announced, "The hosts have arrived."

The warrant served on Bapu was somewhat odd. It ordered the arrest of Bapu, Miraben, and Uncle. But Ba and Pyarelalji were given the choice to come with Bapu or not.*

Ba asked Bapu, "What does this order mean?"

Bapu explained it to her. Then he asked, "What do you want to do?"

We all believed that this time in prison would be the final one. Miraben was pleased to be able to share it with Bapu. But Ba was perplexed. She said to Bapu, "You tell me what to do."

*Miraben was Gandhi's British disciple and colleague, Madeleine Slade. Pyarelal Nayyar was Gandhi's second secretary.

Bapu said, "Since you ask, I'd like you to get arrested separately by speaking in my place at the rally scheduled for this evening. But, if you want to come with me, I won't object. If they arrest you separately, they may keep you apart from me. You must consider all this and decide."

It was no easy choice. On one hand was their lifelong relationship. It was not certain Bapu would survive this prison term. And even visiting Bapu might not be possible. On the other hand were Bapu's own wishes.

Yet Ba made her decision in less time than it has taken to tell. She said resolutely, "As for me, I would like to be with you in this hour. But, even more, I want to fulfill your wishes. So I will stay."

I began to pack for Uncle. I had often said to him, "Uncle, you never do any original writing. Whatever you write is either a transcription of Bapu's speeches or a translation of a book." Smiling, Uncle would reply, "Original writing, I'll leave to you." But then he would tell me how he had plots for five or six novels ready in his mind. If he ever got a long vacation—in other words, a long prison term—he would write them down. He also wanted to translate into Gujarati some songs of Gurudev Rabindranath Tagore.*

For a number of months, I had kept a copy of those songs ready at hand, along with five or six pads of paper. Now I brought them to Uncle and asked, "I should pack these too, shouldn't I?"

But Uncle was indifferent. He said, "You don't need to

---

*A great poet, artist, philosopher, and educator of India, contemporary to Gandhi. *Gurudev* means "Great Teacher."

pack anything like that. Bapu's fast is hanging over my head. If he fasts this time, the government may let him die. I'm not going to live to see all this. I don't know if I'll last even a week in prison."

I said, "Don't say such things."

Uncle didn't reply.

Before going with the police, Bapu said prayers. The atmosphere was charged. Bapu had already declared that, after his arrest, each Indian would become a leader and with nonviolence firmly in mind should take initiative in the struggle against the government. He had predicted the struggle would be short and swift. We were all greatly excited.

The four were brought to the police car. As Uncle was about to get in, I told him, "We will meet again in free India!"

In reply, Uncle kissed my cheek.

That was my last kiss from Uncle.

Uncle died on the morning of August 15, 1942, within six days of entering the Aga Khan palace.* Mother and I were not informed by government officials, though they knew we were at Sevagram. We learned of it the next day, from friends who had heard it on the radio.

At the time of Uncle's cremation, Bapu sent us a telegram. It took three weeks to arrive at Sevagram. It said, "Mahadev died yogi's, patriot's death." Perhaps the contents explains why it was held up so long. In an attached

---

*The Aga Khan was a Muslim hierarch. His palace—in Poona, near Bombay—was requisitioned by the British for use as a prison.

letter, a government official expressed regret at the "inadvertent" delay.

At this point, Mother and I asked to visit Bapu. Permission was denied. We were given no information on where Uncle had been cremated. Even his ashes were denied us.

But we had come to know that Uncle had been cremated at the palace itself. We also learned that Bapu visited the spot twice daily, to lay flowers on it. Later, we received from Bapu some ashes he had preserved.

For Mother and me, the void left by Uncle's death could not be filled. For years, we suffered from his loss. Besides our love for him, he had been our sole support.

Yet never for a moment were we bitter toward the government. We felt it was all just part of the struggle against British rule. Willingness to sacrifice without resentment was the beauty of nonviolent struggle. In fact, I felt a kind of pride that Uncle had died in prison.

When Bapu started his prison fast,* Mother and I again asked to visit him. This time we were told it would be allowed. But we had to agree to stay on as prisoners and forego contact with the outside. We accepted the conditions.

A barbed wire fence, eleven feet high, had been set up around the entire palace. Seventy-six gunmen were on guard, day and night.

Bapu's cot had been placed halfway along the palace's long verandah. It was the seventh day of his fast. When we

---

*Gandhi never carried out his plan to fast on entering the prison. The fast referred to here took place the following February.

bowed to him, the tears Mother had held back for six long months rushed out.

Bapu tried to say something. "Mahadev..." But his voice choked on this first word, and tears filled his eyes. It was the first time I had seen Bapu cry.

We remained in the palace another three weeks, but seldom talked to Bapu. However, I had almost continual talks with Pyarelalji. It was from these talks that I first discovered Bapu did not approve of the widespread acts of sabotage against government property.*

I had been in favor of such actions. I too had planned to burn mailboxes on dark nights, in the company of a local gang armed with bamboo knives. One in the gang had begun talk of carrying a revolver. I had at once been on my guard. I had told him firmly that there was no place in nonviolence for a revolver.

Yet I had believed that, short of destroying life or private property, there was no act that nonviolence ruled out. I had been glad to read about telephone lines being cut and railroad tracks being pulled up.

In several parts of the country, campaigns of sabotage had delivered the government into the hands of the people. I had felt proud at such news. I had myself begun to establish contacts with gangs of saboteurs. I had published underground bulletins. In all this, I believed I was acting as Bapu would wish.

All this I told Pyarelalji. He patiently listened to all of it. Not only patiently, but sympathetically. Yet gradually he tried to show me how damage to any property was violent,

---

*These acts started as soon as Gandhi was imprisoned. Because the British held him incommunicado, Gandhi was powerless to halt them.

how any secrecy hurt a nonviolent struggle. Violence was the government's way, not ours.

I slowly came to understand that the path I had favored was wrong. But I did not feel guilty about it. Bapu had labelled our lapses in past campaigns as follies. He had tried to find a way to bring the country back onto the right track. But he had not denounced the errors of any who acted out of love for India. Because of this, the ordinary Indian was still willing to accept Bapu's guidance.

We had much free time in the palace. I was using mine to read an English translation of Victor Hugo's *Les Miserables*. Bapu was surprised to hear of it. He called me to him and complimented me. I felt bashful.

Pyarelalji told Bapu, "You still think of him as little Babla. But he discusses the national situation with me. We've been having an involved debate on nonviolence."

Bapu said, "Oh, I know. Even as a small child, he loved to argue. But, this time, what surprised me was his command of English."

He turned to me and said, "Since you were discussing nonviolence, you should know that my own idea of it has evolved. Earlier I believed that, if there were violence in one part of the country, it would not allow the use of nonviolence anywhere. Today, I believe that nonviolence must shed its small light in the midst of even the fiercest storm of violence."

I write these lines as we approach 1969, centenary year of Bapu's birth. It is a quarter century since Uncle passed away.

What is a quarter century, or a century, in the passage of eternity? Yet, even a moment's encounter with the righteous—face to face, or in remembrances such as these—can be a boat that carries you across the sea of life.

Index

The Peacewatch Editions

☐ GANDHI'S SEVEN STEPS TO GLOBAL CHANGE. By Guy de Mallac. Mahatma Gandhi's principles for political and social transformation are spelled out for the first time in this information-packed handbook. A must for peacemakers! $6.50.

☐ PEACE PILGRIM: Her Life and Work in Her Own Words. The inspirational and practical peacemaking classic by America's wandering saint. (Over a quarter million copies in print!) $8.00 (paperbound); $14.95 (hardcover).

☐ VICTORIES WITHOUT VIOLENCE. By Ruth A. Fry. More than 70 true incidents of ordinary people coming through dangerous situations without using physical force. $6.00.

☐ A ROAD TO THE FUTURE. By Mikhail S. Gorbachev. Complete text of the Soviet leader's world-changing 1988 address to the United Nations — the speech that ended the Cold War! $5.95.

☐ PEACE LIKE A RIVER: A Personal Journey. By Sue Guist. Intimate account of a nine month walk across America in the search for global peace. $8.95.

☐ THE GREAT PEACE MARCH: An American Odyssey. By Franklin Folsom & Connie Fledderjohann. Complete account of the 1986 walk from Los Angeles to Washington to end the nuclear arms race. Many photographs and appendices. $10.95.

☐ GANDHI THROUGH A CHILD'S EYES: An Intimate Memoir. By Narayan Desai. A boy who lived in the Mahatma's household during the struggle for India's independence offers a beautiful and revealing portrait. $8.00.

- -

OCEAN TREE BOOKS
Post Office Box 1295, Santa Fe, New Mexico 87504 USA
Telephone: (505) 983-1412

☐ Please send me the Peacewatch Editions books checked above. (Enclose $2.00 for postage and packing for the first book, and 50 cents for each additional book. Checks should be payable to Ocean Tree Books.)

Name _____

Address _____

City _____ State _____

Zip Code _____